KETO MEAL PREP

Cookbook for Beginners

High-Fat and Low-Carb Recipes
for Busy People on the Keto Diet

Davina Eason

Warning-Disclaimer

The purpose of this book is to educate and entertain. The author or publisher does not guarantee that anyone following the techniques, suggestions, ideas, or strategies will become successful. The author and publisher shall have neither liability or responsibility to anyone with respect to any loss or damage caused, or alleged to be caused, directly or indirectly by the information contained in this book.

CONTENTS

SNACKS & SIDE DISHES

VEGAN & VEGETARIAN 80

DESSERTS 92

MEASUREMENT CONVERSION TABLES 96

RECIPE INDEX 97

INTRODUCTION

I started to notice that my life life has become dominated by activities revolving around working and organizing food, and a typical week, consisted of waking up in the morning, rushing to work, commuting, working, having hasty lunch break, commuting back home, cooking dinner, running errands, etc. And not much time left for anything else. What about all money flowing out of your wallet to satisfy my food whims, or just save me some time to enjoy my favorite youtube channels?

I couldn't resist buying from a burger stand or dropping in to a bakery for a quick slice of pizza? The world doesn't end if you do so once in a while, but if added up, you know you are spending lots of money on stuff you could easily do without.

Yeah, that's life, but one thing is for sure - it does't take much to make it way better. Planning meals in an organized way for the whole week (or more) may sound like a big investment, but in reality, it saves us a lot of time and money. How much happier would your family, partner, or friends then be? How much would you develop yourself, having more time to follow a passion or hobby? How much more money would there be left in your pocket if you stopped spending it randomly whenever you have a whim.

By no means this isn't a conventional cookbook. Our world is accelerating and new forms of cooking are coming out. This book is a healthy culinary response to that acceleration and modern people's needs. So, let's begin.

HOW THIS COOKBOOK WILL HELP YOU?

Meal prep is a process that will be thoroughly explained in the pages of this cookbook, as well as how to follow the Keto Diet. You will learn how to organize yourself, get everything ready and what is the actual cooking process like.

This book will explain how to get on this journey without feeling overwhelmed or unmotivated. Next, you will learn everything you need to know about the Ketogenic Diet, it's pros and cons. It will aslo give you the reasons why your Instant Pot pressure cooker will take your meal prep to the next level, and how you can use it to create awesome, delicious and easy keto meals.

And at the end, you will be presented with plenty of exciting and inspiring keto diet meal prep recipes that will cover all your daily meals and needs, taking you to the extraordinary lifystyle you have always wished for.

MEAL PREP - THE BASICS?

Quick fix in the modern age

So what exactly is Meal Prep or Meal Preparation? It's about cooking dishes in advance for a few days or for a week in order to save time and streamline your healthy eating habits. Major idea is to cook a big portion of one kind of food and divided it into parts, pack into plastic containers and store in the fridge or freezer.

It's practical for everyone: busy people find it easier to cook dinner once a week, because they simply have too tight schedule during the week-days; sportsmen cook in advance in order to control intakes of fats, proteins, carbohydrates; dieting individuals monitors their calories intake; people on a low budget prefer Meal Prep, because it is the most economical way of eating. This list can be endless because Meal Prep is a versatile tool to schedule your breakfast, lunches and dinners, as well as make your nutrition more wholesome.

Meal Prep will make your evenings better: instead of cooking your dinner after work, you can enjoy tasty food as soon as you cross the threshold of your home.

HOW CAN MEAL PREP CHANGE YOUR LIFE?

Planning is winning

One very big advantage of Meal Prep is that you learn how to organize your day better.

How to starts? First off, plan your shopping carefully. If you have never used shopping lists before, it's perhaps time to start. That will help you adjust meals and portions accordingly. You will learn how to prepare and eat just enough without having leftovers or overeating.

If you prepare meals for the whole family, you will save yourself the trouble of preparing different food two or even three times a day and then cleaning it all up. The alternative beign eating out, and that's expensive and most of the time - unhealthy.

Also, planning your meals develops you as a person because once taken care of, that skill may go beyond cooking and will surely help you organize your life better.

Long-Term Weight Loss is Finally Around the Corner

When you have the whole-day schedule prepared, you are less likely to snack outside the schedule. Having a general plan for anything in life strongly builds a sense of discipline.

Consequently, if you combine meal prepping with appropriate nutrition, you will create an excellent lifestyle where weight loss is not a goal itself, but merely a means to an end. You will not have to obsessively focus on counting, yet you will see results soon enough. No more calories count, weight loss, or how I refere to it as stay fit, will be easier than ever.

At the end, losing weight happens automatically as a side effect of eating appropriate, schedule-based meals.

Simple & Healthy Plate!

It's very common that through organizing your meals, you greatly decrease the risk of snacking on unhealthy, processed food and fast foods that's literally shouting from every corner of the city.

Many people report that having prepared meals, one quickly notices that even if you fancy some grab-and-go tacos or a burger, you will not go for it. Getting food from vending machines will also become a thing of the past. And, of course, you are much less likely to throw out something you spent time and money on.

That's why you will quickly realize that meal prep makes you a healthier person. When you eat cleaner, you feel better, more energetic, disciplines and you not only have a sense of control over your life, but also this type of food prepping, is a the key to long-term happiness. Think of the food as your fuel and of yourself as a top class luxurious car. Would you fuel it with low-quality gas that could damage the engine? Probably not. Meal prepping forces you to skip low-quality fuel and treat your engine better.

The key is in the Balance

In order to become an excellent meal planner, basic knowledge about food will come in very handy. Knowing how to compose a balanced meal is not that difficult. A proper content of proteins, fats, and carbohydrates in an adequate ratio will help you remain satiated for a longer period of time. As a result, hunger pangs will diminish and you will stop snacking on foods your body doesn't really need.

All these leads to developing a genuine interest in healthy eating habits, as well as how to pack and store food properly. Simple as it sounds, a bit of know-how is necessary.

Last but not least, labelling pre-made meals will keep your food organized and make sure you have control over the freshness. Meal prepping does not mean eating stale food.

MY TOP 8 TIPS TO GET STARTED

1. **PICK UP A DAY AND STICK TO IT**

   Monday or Sunday are considered among the best days to prepare food for the whole week. Draw up a list of meals and days, and have it on a piece of paper. That never fails. You can easily print meal planners from the internet, which may be an excellent solution here.Better yet, learn to plan two or even three weeks ahead and you find the perfect balance and meal prepping days for you.

2. **TRY AS MANY DIFFERENT FOODS AS POSSIBLE**

   What that means is not repeating the same dish seven times a week. That would be too boring and unhealthy at the same time. Prepare two to three alternatives so you avoid nutritional burn-out. It may be something as simple as changing the source of proteins (i.e. meat for fish or tofu) or a different type of vegetables.

3. **TIME FOR A SHOPPING LIST**

   Not only it will save you precious efforts, but it will also train you to stick to the plan, not toss impulse items into your cart. You will save money and time and keep yourself from buying junk food, however crispy it may be. If something's not in your fridge, you will not eat it.

4. **START SMALL, THEN GO BIG**

   As every beginner, your safest bet is starting small. Although trying more difficult recipes is most welcome, I recommend that at the beginning you stick to simple recipes. Over time, as you become more adept, you may increase the complexity or try your own recipes.

5. **QUANTITY IS IMPORTANT**

   Why not prepare a couple more things in the oven or on the stove. It's not only time saving, but your electricity bill will look way better.

6. **GO FOR THE BEST STORAGE.**

High quality containers and mason jars will help you store things longer without risk of wasting food. It may even make food taste better. I would also recommend buying larger pots and frying pans.

7. SAVE EVEN MORE TIME BUYING PRE-CUT VEGGIES

Yes, I know. They are more expensive. But even despite that fact, they make your life easier and will save you additional time and efforts, which is important in the long-term.

8. GOOD OLD WATER

Though obvious, we often confuse hunger pangs with dehydration. Water fills your stomach and **you do not feel hunger, which makes it a real basis of each diet.**

FOODS AND PRODUCTS TO AVOID

- Processed foods like pasta, rice, pizzas
- Soft drinks and sugary beverages
- All kinds of crackers, cookies, cakes, and pastries that are not keto
- Candy bars, energy drinks and traditional ice creams
- All kinds of fast foods, including trational wheat bread
- MSG and other toxic additives

It seems difficult until you've done it.

The whole idea of the meal prep is to maintain a healthy lifestyle in a rushing environment. It offers the wisdom of not taking the easy way out and eating junk food tempting us everywhere we go. Instead, we learn to take responsibility for what we eat and what we become as a result. Given this, the Keto diet offers one of the best posibilities to eat healthy without losing time and energy cooking every day, even twice a day.

The keto recipes here are meant to help you initiate the changes and go through the tough beginning. But remember, things seem dificult until you make them seem easy. The results will be well worth the time. No doubt about it.

With this book, you make an investment that will pay huge interests without forcing you to spend tons of money. It's really simple to follow and the results are guaranteed.

Your success is entirely dependent on your determination to stick to the plan and give up on toxic things you considered normal before.

The Keto Meal Prep Recipes in the book are easy and simple for beginners. Advanced cooking freaks will definitely find something for themselves as well.

In order to take any action, we first need to realize the importance of our diet and how it affects our bodies. Love the life you have while enjoying the journey to a better and healthier nutrition.

THE KETO DIET

Undoubtedly the most controversial today, the Ketogenic diet holds tons of successful stories that prove to us that the secret to healthy living and weight maintaining indeed lies in ditching the carbs, many people are scared to approach such a strict eating plan.

Will I be feeling bad? Carbs give me energy! Won't all that fat raise my cholesterol levels? Won't butter and bacon widen my waist? Will I hurt my health if I enter ketosis? The answer? A definite **NO**.

Oh It won't work for me!

Again, not true. Ask anyone who has been motivated enough to stick to this diet's guidelines and you will get the same answer – the Keto diet will help you lose or maintain weight in the healthiest way possible without sacrificing your full tummy or your satisfied taste buds.

You may think the he main point of the Ketogenic diet is to starve you to death, but that's not the case. The Keto diet stands for a lifestyle clear of carbohydrates which will train your body to run on fat. It may seem impossible at this point, but this is very achievable.

To undrerstand it, think of your body as a car with a backup tank. When the petrol runs out, your car will use the fuel from the gas tank to keep on moving. Your body works in a similar way. Once you empty your glucose reserves (as we know that carbohydrates get broken down into glucose), your body will turn to your reserved fat for energy.

Ketosis - Healthy or Dangerous?

So what is ketosis? It is the moment that your body starts to use fat for energy. During the food conversion fat gets broken down into ketones (hence the name ketogenic), and the goal of this diet is to use the ketones for energy instead of glucose.

Many confuse the state of ketosis with diabetic ketosis, which is something else entirely, and think that it is dangerous. Instead, it is just an indicator that your carb ditching has not been in vain and that you are on the right path to weight loss and lasting health.

Signs Keto Diet Works for You

Reaching ketosis is the goal of the Keto diet. That's the ultimate YES that you have been following the right Ketogenic guidelines. You will know that you are in the state of ketosis if you are experiencing fatigue, rapid weight loss, or just a bad breath.

These symptoms may not sound appealing but they will only bother you for about 2 weeks or so, since that is the average time that the human body needs in order to adapt to the new source of energy.

Keto Macros?

The Ketogenic diet has gotten the bad reputation for being hard to follow thanks to its strict macro recommendation:

70% **Fats**

20-25 % **Protein**

5-10% **Carbs**

While it's difficult to accomplish on daily basis, if you know which ingredients to amount to which macros, the Ketogenic diet is pretty straightforward and easy plan to follow.

WHAT TO FOODS TO EAT AND FOODS TO AVOID

Foods to Eat

- Meat (fresh and processed meat), Seafood, Eggs
- All Dairy Products (milk, cheeses, heavy cream, sour cream, yogurt, butter, etc.)
- Avocados (low in carbs, high in healthy fats)
- Non Starchy Veggies (broccoli, leafy greens, cauliflower, asparagus, Brussel sprouts, zucchini, cabbage, tomatoes, etc.)
- Lower-in-carbs Fruits (Berries, watermelon, citrus fruits, etc.)
- Seeds, Nuts and Healthy oils (such as olive oil, coconut oil, flaxseed oil, etc.)

Foods to Avoid

- Grains, Beans and Legumes
- Sugar, Trans Fats and Fruit Juices
- Starchy Veggies (corn, potatoes, peas, parsnips, etc.)
- Diet Soda, Refined Gats and Oils (such as margarine)

BREAKFAST

Homemade Ham & Cheese Crepes

Prep + Cooking time: 30 minutes | Servings: 4

Ingredients

2 tbsp butter

2 eggs

1 cup almond milk

½ cup almond flour

1 tsp allspice

Salt and black pepper, to taste

1 cup cheddar cheese, shredded

8 thin ham slices

Directions

In a bowl, beat the eggs, allspice, salt, pepper, almond flour, and almond milk. Heat a pan over medium heat, brush with some butter and add in a ladle of the batter, spreading it evenly. Cook for 2 minutes.

Flip, spread ¼ of the cheese and top with 2 ham slices. Cook for another minute until golden.

Roll up the crepe and set aside. Repeat with the remaining batter, brushing the pan with butter between each crepe.

Per serving

Calories 307; Fat: 22.7g; Net Carbs: 5.1g; Protein: 20.7g

Storing

Place the crepes in a resealable container and store for up to 5 days at room temperature. To freeze, place in Ziploc bags for up to 3 months. Defrost at room temperature.

Easy Rosemary Focaccia

Prep + Cooking time: 25 minutes | Servings: 4

Ingredients

2 tbsp olive oil

½ cup almond flour

5 large eggs

½ cup water

¼ cup flax seed meal

¼ cup chia seed meal

1 tsp garlic powder

8 fresh rosemary sprigs

Directions

In a bowl, combine the almond flour, eggs, water, flax seed meal, chia seed meal, garlic powder, and rosemary.

Grease a baking sheet with olive oil and spread the batter. With your fingers, do dimples on top and scatter the rosemary over.

Drizzle with olive oil and bake in the oven for 20 minutes until golden, at 400 F.

Per serving

Calories 152, Fat 12.8g; Net Carbs 1g; Protein 8g

Storing

Place the cups in a resealable container and store for up to 7 days at room temperature. To freeze, place in Ziploc bags for up to 3 months. Defrost at room temperature.

Quick Breakfast Egg Muffins

Prep + Cooking time: 20 minutes | Servings: 6

Ingredients

4 tbsp xylitol

6 oz cream cheese

¼ cup sour cream

3 eggs, beaten

¼ cup raspberries

½ tsp vanilla extract

⅓ tsp ground cinnamon

Directions

Set oven to 360 degrees F and coat a muffin pan with cooking spray.

Mix all ingredients in a bowl. Split the batter into the muffin cups and bake for 12 to 15 minutes.

Remove and set on a wire rack to cool slightly before storing.

Per serving

Calories 139; Fat: 11.2g; Net Carbs: 4.1g; Protein: 5.2g

Storing

Divide between airtight containers and put in the fridge. You can use them for up to 7 days. To freeze, transfer to Ziploc bags and freeze up to 3 months. Defrost in the microwave for a couple of minutes.

Italian Sausage & Gorgonzola Goffres

Prep + Cooking time: 20 minutes | Servings: 4

Ingredients

4 tbsp olive oil
Salt and black pepper, to taste
4 tbsp almond milk
½ tsp basil, chopped
½ tsp chili pepper flakes
8 eggs
½ cup gorgonzola cheese, crumbled
2 cooked Italian sausage links, chopped
2 tbsp fresh chives, chopped

Directions

In a mixing bowl, whisk the eggs, almond milk, olive oil, chili pepper flakes, black pepper, and salt. Gently fold in the gorgonzola cheese, sausage and basil, until well incorporated.

Preheat a waffle iron, pour in one cup of the batter, close and cook for 5 minutes or until golden-brown. Do the same with the rest of the batter.

Per serving

Calories 382; Fat: 30.8g; Net Carbs: 3.6g; Protein: 22g

Storing

When cooled, divide between airtight containers and put in the fridge. Use them for up to 7 days. To freeze, transfer to Ziploc bags and freeze up to 3 months. Defrost in the microwave for a couple of minutes.

Cheesy Zucchini Balls with Turkey Bacon

Prep + Cooking time: 30 minutes | Servings: 4

Ingredients

1 cup turkey bacon, chopped

2 zucchinis, squeezed and grated

½ cup feta cheese, crumbled

½ cup cream cheese

½ cup Gruyère cheese

½ cup dill pickles, chopped, squeezed

1 cup grated Parmesan cheese

½ tsp dill seeds

¼ tsp dried dill weed

½ tsp onion powder

Salt and black pepper, to taste

1 cup pork rinds, crushed

Directions

Preheat the oven to 420 degrees F and grease a baking dish with cooking spray.

In a bowl, mix feta cheese, a ½ cup of Parmesan cheese, cream cheese, zucchinis, dill pickles, turkey bacon, and Gruyère cheese until well combined. Roll into balls and set aside.

In a large plate, combine the remaining Parmesan cheese, pork rinds, dill weed, black pepper, onion powder, dill seeds, and salt. Coat the balls in the Parmesan mixture.

Arrange on the baking dish and bake in the oven for 15-20 minutes until browned on all sides. Let cool completely before storing.

Per serving

Calories 464; Fat: 35.8g; Net Carbs: 6.8g; Protein: 27.5g

Storing

Divide between 4 airtight containers and put in the fridge. You can use them for up to 5 days. To freeze, transfer to Ziploc bags and freeze up to 2 months. Defrost in the microwave for a couple of minutes.

Egg Cups with Parma Ham

Prep + Cooking time: 40 minutes | Servings: 6

Ingredients

12 oz Parma ham, chopped

6 eggs

¼ cup Parmesan cheese, grated

2 tbsp almond flour

2 tbsp mayonnaise

¼ tsp garlic powder

1 shallot, chopped

Sea salt to taste

Directions

Preheat oven to 375 degrees F and treat a muffin pan with cooking spray.

Mix together the Parma ham, shallot, eggs, garlic powder, salt, mayonnaise, almond flour, and Parmesan cheese in a bowl.

Fill each cup two-thirds full with the mixture and bake in the oven for 20-25 minutes until the tops are firm to the touch. Leave to cool before storing.

Per serving

Calories 170, Fat: 8.5g; Net Carbs: 5.4g; Protein: 17.3g

Storing

Place the cups in a resealable container and store for up to 5 days at room temperature. To freeze, place in Ziploc bags for up to 3 months. Defrost at room temperature.

Creole Chicken Stew

Prep + Cooking time: 40 minutes | Servings: 4

Ingredients

1 pound chicken breasts, cubed

1 stick celery, chopped

6 tbsp creole seasoning

2 tbsp dried oregano

2 bell peppers, seeded and chopped

1 onion, chopped

2 tomatoes, chopped

32 oz chicken broth

2 tbsp garlic powder

2 tbsp chili powder

Salt and black pepper, to taste

3 tbsp olive oil

Directions

Place a pot over medium heat and warm olive oil. Add the onion, celery, bell peppers, salt, oregano, garlic powder, cayenne, and creole seasoning and cook for 3-4 minutes.

Add the remaining ingredients and bring to a boil. Reduce the heat and simmer for 20 minutes, covered.

Per serving

Calories 287, Fat 20.5g; Net Carbs 5.3g; Protein 17.5g

Storing

Divide the salad between 4 airtight containers and put in the fridge. You can use them for up to 3 days. To freeze, transfer to Ziploc bags and freeze up to 3 months. Defrost in the microwave for a couple of minutes.

Chicken Stuffed Mushrooms with Almonds

Prep + Cooking time: 40 minutes | Servings: 6

Ingredients

3 cups cauliflower florets
Salt and black pepper, to taste
2 leeks, chopped
1 ½ pounds ground chicken
2 tbsp butter
1 tbsp olive oil
10 portobello mushrooms, stems removed
½ cup vegetable broth
1 tbsp thyme
2 tbsp almonds, crumbled

Directions

Preheat oven to 350 degrees F. In a food processor, add the cauliflower florets, black pepper and salt. Pulse a few times and transfer to a plate.

Set a pan over medium heat and warm the butter, stir in the leeks and thyme and cook for 3 minutes. Add in the cauliflower rice and ground chicken, and cook for 3-5 minutes. Season with salt and black pepper.

Rub the mushrooms with olive oil and arrange them on a lined baking sheet. Stuff each one with chicken mixture, top with chopped almonds and put in the oven. Bake for 30 minutes.

Per serving

Calories 355, Fat 23.8g; Net Carbs 6.9g; Protein 29.4g

Storing

Divide between airtight containers. Place in the fridge and consume within 3 days. To freeze, transfer to Ziploc bags and freeze up to 3 months. Defrost in the microwave for a couple of minutes to enjoy.

Parsnip Chicken Bake

Prep + Cooking time: 55 minutes | Servings: 4

Ingredients

1 pound parsnips, quartered lengthways

3 tbsp olive oil

10 oz shallots, halved

1 pound zucchinis, cubed

Salt and black pepper, to taste

2 garlic cloves

1 pound chicken thighs

Directions

Preheat oven to 350 degrees F.

In a baking dish, arrange the parsnips, shallots, garlic cloves, and butternut squash. Drizzle with some olive oil and bake in the oven for 20 minutes.

Meanwhile, set a pan over medium heat and warm the remaining olive oil. Place in the chicken thighs, season with black pepper and salt, and cook each side for 3 minutes until golden.

Lay them over the vegetables. If necessary add a little bit of water. Bake for another 5-10 minutes until the chicken is cooked through.

Per serving

Calories 502, Fat 31g Net Carbs 11.2g; Protein 23.9g

Storing

When cooled, divide between 4 airtight containers. Place in the fridge and consume within 3-4 days. To freeze, transfer to Ziploc bags and freeze up to 3 months. Defrost in the microwave for a couple of minutes.

Chicken Meatloaf with Cheesy Filling

Prep + Cooking time: 50 minutes | Servings: 8

Ingredients

8 oz tomato sauce, sugar-free

2 lb ground chicken

2 tbsp fresh parsley, chopped

3 garlic cloves, minced

1 onion, chopped

Salt and ground black pepper, to taste

1 cup Colby cheese, shredded

½ cup cottage cheese

1 cup Grana Padano cheese, grated

1 green onion, chopped

Directions

Preheat oven to 380 degrees F.

In a bowl, combine the chicken with half of the tomato sauce, black pepper, onion, salt, and garlic. In a separate bowl, combine the cottage cheese with half of the Grana Padano cheese, green onion, black pepper, half of the Colby cheese, salt, and parsley.

Place half of the chicken mixture into a loaf pan, and spread evenly. Place in cheese filling and spread evenly. Top with the rest of the meat mixture and spread again. Set the meatloaf in the oven and bake for 25 minutes.

Remove meatloaf from the oven, then spread the rest of the tomato sauce, Grana Padano cheese and Colby cheese, and bake for 18 minutes. Allow meatloaf cooling. With a sharp knife cut into slices.

Per serving

Calories 391 Fat 26.6g; Net Carbs 5.5g; Protein 30.7 g

Storing

Divide the meatloaf slices between 8 airtight containers. Place in the fridge and consume within 3 days.

Italian Baked Chicken

Prep + Cooking time: 60 minutes | Servings: 4

Ingredients

1 pound chicken breasts, boneless, halved
½ cup mayonnaise
½ cup sour cream
1 cup cherry tomatoes
Salt and black pepper, to taste
¾ cup Pecorino Toscano cheese, grated
8 mozzarella cheese slices
1 garlic clove, minced

Directions

Preheat oven to 370 degrees F.

Add the chicken breasts to an oiled baking dish, and top 2 mozzarella cheese slices to each piece.

In a bowl, combine the Pecorino Toscano cheese, black pepper, sour cream, mayonnaise, salt, and garlic. Sprinkle this over the chicken, and set the dish in the oven. Bake for 1 hour.

Per serving

Calories 654, Fat 51.5g; Net Carbs 5.7g; Protein 44.4g

Storing

When cooled, divide between 4 airtight containers and place in the fridge. Use them for up to 3 days. To freeze, transfer to Ziploc bags and freeze up to 3 months. Defrost in the microwave for a few minutes.

One-Pot Green Chicken Breasts

Prep + Cooking time: 25 minutes | Servings: 4

Ingredients

2 chicken breasts, skinless, boneless, cut into strips
1 tbsp butter
1 tsp red pepper flakes
1 tbsp fresh ginger, grated
¼ cup tamari sauce
½ tsp garlic powder
½ cup water
½ cup xylitol
½ tsp xanthan gum
A bunch of spring onions, chopped
1 small head broccoli, cut into florets

Directions

Cook the chicken and ginger in melted butter over medium heat for 4 minutes.

Stir in the water, pepper flakes, garlic powder, tamari sauce, xanthan gum, and xylitol, and cook for 15 minutes.

Add in the green onions and broccoli, and cook for 6 minutes.

Per serving

Calories 338, Fat 16.5g; Net Carbs 1.6g; Protein 33.8g

Storing

Divide between 4 airtight containers and put in the fridge. You can use them for up to 3 days. To freeze, transfer to Ziploc bags and freeze up to 3 months. Defrost in the microwave for a few minutes to enjoy.

Cottage & Spinach Chicken Rolls

Prep + Cooking time: 25 minutes | Servings: 4

Ingredients

2 cups baby spinach, cooked and chopped

4 chicken breasts

4 ounces dry white wine

Salt and black pepper, to taste

4 ounces cream cheese, softened

4 ounces cottage cheese, crumbled

1 garlic clove, minced

1 tbsp canola oil

2 tbsp oregano

Directions

Preheat oven to 420 degrees F.

In a bowl, combine the cottage cheese with cream cheese, salt and pepper, garlic, oregano, and baby spinach.

Put the chicken breasts on a working surface, cut a pocket in each, and stuff with the spinach mixture.

Set a pan over medium heat and warm oil. Add the stuffed chicken, and cook each side for 2 minutes.

Put in a baking tray, drizzle with white wine and 2 tablespoons of water and then bake in the oven for 10 minutes. Allow to cool completely before storing.

Per serving

Calories 514, Fat 32.4g; Net Carbs 2.3g; Protein 51g

Storing

When cooled, divide between 4 airtight containers. Place in the fridge and consume within 3-4 days. To freeze, transfer to Ziploc bags and freeze up to 3 months. Defrost in the microwave for a few minutes.

Kielbasa & Cheddar Chicken

Prep + Cooking time: 40 minutes | Servings: 4

Ingredients

1 tbsp olive oil

2 cans (6-ounce) tomato sauce

4 chicken breast halves, skinless and boneless

Salt and black pepper, to taste

1 tsp dried majoran

4 oz cheddar cheese, sliced

1 tsp garlic powder

2 oz kielbasa, sliced

Directions

Rub the chicken all over with the majoran, salt, garlic powder, and black pepper.

In a pan over medium heat, warm olive oil. Add in the chicken, cook each side for 2 minutes, and remove to a baking dish.

Top with the cheddar cheese slices, spread the sauce, then cover with kielbasa slices. Bake for 30 minutes at 390 degrees F.

Per serving

Calories 515, Fat 35.5g; Net Carbs 1.7g; Protein 45g

Storing

Divide between 4 airtight containers. Place in the fridge for up to 3 days. To freeze, transfer to Ziploc bags and freeze up to 3 months. Defrost in the microwave and microwave for a couple of minutes to enjoy.

Chicken Breasts with Green Topping

Prep + Cooking time: 60 minutes | Servings: 4

Ingredients

½ cup mascarpone cheese

1 pound chicken breasts, skinless and boneless

8 oz canned asparagus, chopped

1 cup collard greens

½ cup Pecorino cheese, grated

1 tbsp onion powder

1 tbsp garlic powder

Salt and black pepper, to taste

½ cup mozzarella cheese, shredded

Directions

Preheat oven to 350 degrees F. Lay the chicken breasts on a lined baking sheet, season with black pepper and salt, set in the oven and bake for 35 minutes.

In a bowl, combine the asparagus with onion powder, Pecorino cheese, salt, collard greens, mascarpone cheese, garlic powder, and black pepper.

Remove the chicken from the oven, and cut each piece in half. Divide asparagus mixture on top, spread with mozzarella cheese, and bake for another 20 minutes.

Per serving

Calories 345, Fat 22g; Net Carbs 4.6g; Protein 36.7g

Storing

When cooled, divide among 4 airtight containers and place in the fridge. Consume within 3 days. To freeze, transfer to Ziploc bags and freeze up to 3 months. Defrost in the microwave for a few minutes to enjoy.

Crunchy Fried Chicken Strips

Prep + Cooking time: 20 minutes | Servings: 4

Ingredients

3 chicken breasts, cut into strips

4 ounces pork rinds, crushed

2 cups vegetable oil

16 ounces buttermilk

2 eggs, whisked

1 tsp cayenne pepper

Directions

In a dip bowl, combine the chicken breast pieces with pickle juice and refrigerate for 12-24 hours while covered. In a small bowl, mix the pork rinds with cayenne pepper.

Tip the eggs into a separate one. Dip the chicken pieces in the eggs, and then in pork rinds, and ensure they are well coated.

Heat the oil in a high-sided frying pan over medium heat, until sizzling. Fry the chicken for 3 minutes on each side until golden. Remove to paper towels, drain the excess grease, and let cool.

Per serving

Calories 482, Fat 26.4g; Net Carbs 5.7g; Protein 39.2 g

Storing

When cooled, divide between 4 airtight containers and place in the fridge. Consume within 3 days. To freeze, transfer to Ziploc bags and freeze up to 3 months. Defrost in the microwave for a few minutes.

Winter Chicken Stew

Prep + Cooking time: 60 minutes | Servings: 4

Ingredients

2 cups pumpkin, chopped

2 tbsp olive oil

2 celery stalks, chopped

2 cups chicken stock

1 red onion, chopped

1 pound chicken thighs, skinless, boneless

3 garlic cloves, minced

½ tsp dried sage

2 oz sundried tomatoes, chopped

1 cup green beans, frozen

¼ tsp dried thyme

½ cup heavy cream

Salt and black pepper, to taste

A pinch of xanthan gum

Directions

Sauté garlic, pumpkin, celery, and red onion in warm oil over medium heat for 5-6 minutes until tender. Season with salt and pepper.

Stir in the chicken and cook for 5 more minutes.

Pour in the stock, sundried tomatoes, sage and thyme, cover, and cook for 30 minutes.

Remove the cover, stir in xanthan gum, cream, and spinach, and cook for 5 more minutes. Adjust to taste.

Per serving

Calories 412, Fat 31.6g; Net Carbs 5.1g; Protein 20.3g

Storing

When cooled, divide between 4 airtight containers. Place in the fridge and consume within 3 days. To freeze, transfer to Ziploc bags and freeze up to 3 months. Defrost in the microwave for a few minutes.

Stuffed Bell Peppers with Chicken & Cheese

Prep + Cooking time: 25 minutes | Servings: 6

Ingredients

6 bell peppers
2 tbsp olive oil
1 cup cream cheese
¼ cup carrot, chopped
4 tbsp chili sauce
¾ cup gorgonzola cheese, crumbled
1 onion, chopped
½ cup chicken breasts, cooked and chopped
Salt and black pepper, to taste

Directions

Preheat oven to 425 degrees F. In a bowl, combine the gorgonzola cheese with the cream cheese, chicken, onion, carrot, salt, chili sauce, and black pepper.

Cut the tops off the bell peppers and remove the seeds. Stuff each pepper with the mixture, set on a lined baking sheet, place in the oven and bake for 20 minutes.

Per serving

Calories 279, Fat 21.4g; Net Carbs 3.3g; Protein 11.6g

Storing

When cooled, divide between 6 airtight containers and place in the fridge. Consume within 3 days. To freeze, transfer to Ziploc bags and freeze up to 3 months. Defrost in the microwave for a few minutes.

Winter Chicken Legs in Red Sauce

Prep + Cooking time: 1 hour 25 minutes | Servings: 4

Ingredients

2 tbsp ghee
1 pound chicken legs
1 white onion, chopped
2 turnips, chopped
½ pound butternut squash, chopped
2 green bell peppers, cut into chunks
2 cloves garlic, minced
¼ cup coconut flour
1 cup chicken broth
28 oz canned tomato sauce, sugar-free
2 tbsp herbs de provence
Salt and black pepper to taste

Directions

Preheat oven to 400 degrees F. Melt the ghee in a large skillet over medium heat, season the legs with salt and pepper, and fry to brown on both sides for 10 minutes. Remove to a baking dish.

Stir-fry the onion, turnips, bell peppers, squash, and garlic in the same oil, for about 10 minutes.

In a bowl, combine the broth, coconut flour, tomato sauce, and herbs de provence, and pour over the vegetables in the pan. Stir and cook to thicken for 4 minutes. Pour the mixture over the chicken in the baking dish and bake for around 55-60 minutes.

Per serving

Calories 276, Fat 11.3g; Net Carbs 9.2g; Protein 22.6g

Storing

Divide between 4 airtight containers and place in the fridge. Best if consumed within 3 days. To freeze, transfer to Ziploc bags and freeze up to 3 months.

Rolled Chicken Breast with Spinach and Cheese

Prep + Cooking time: 50 minutes | Servings: 4

Ingredients

1 pound chicken breasts, boneless

2 shallots, chopped

½ tsp garlic, minced

2 tbsp butter

2 tbsp olive oil

½ cup mozzarella cheese

1 cup feta cheese, crumbled

12 oz spinach, chopped

A pinch of nutmeg

Salt and black pepper to taste

Directions

In a skillet over medium heat, melt the butter, and sauté shallots, garlic, and spinach for 5-6 minutes, until tender. Season with salt and black pepper, and set aside to cool slightly.

Pound the chicken until it doubles in size. Mix the feta cheese, spinach mixture, mozzarella cheese, and nutmeg in a bowl.

Divide the mixture between the chicken breasts and spread it out evenly. Wrap the chicken in a plastic wrap and refrigerate for 15 minutes.

Meanhwhile, preheat the oven to 370 degrees F.

In a pan over medium heat, warm the olive oil. Add the rolls and cook 4-5 on all sides.

Transfer them to a lined baking sheet, add in a cup of water, and bake for 20 minutes. Let cool before storing.

Per serving

Calories 453, Fat: 31.3g; Net Carbs: 4.6g; Protein: 36.3g

Storing

Divide between 4 airtight containers. Place in the fridge and consume within 3 days. To freeze, transfer to Ziploc bags and freeze up to 3 months. Defrost in the microwave for a couple of minutes to enjoy.

Chicken Breasts Stuffed with Parma Ham

Prep + Cooking time: 40 minutes | Servings: 4

Ingredients

4 chicken breasts
2 tbsp olive oil
3 cloves garlic, minced
3 shallots, finely chopped
4 tbsp dried mixed herbs
8 slices Parma ham
8 oz cream cheese
2 lemons, zested
Salt and black pepper to taste

Directions

Preheat the oven to 350 degrees F. Heat the oil in a small skillet and sauté the garlic and shallots with a pinch of salt and lemon zest, for 3 minutes. Turn the heat off and let it cool.

After, stir the cream cheese and mixed herbs into the shallot mixture.

Score a pocket in each chicken breast, fill the holes with the cream cheese mixture and cover with the cut-out chicken.

Wrap each breast with two Parma ham slices and secure the ends with a toothpick. Lay the chicken parcels on a greased baking sheet and cook in the oven for 20 minutes.

Per serving

Calories 636, Fat 44g; Net Carbs 7.3g; Protein 50g

Storing

When cooled, divide among 4 airtight containers. Place in the fridge. You can use them for up to 3 days. To freeze, transfer to Ziploc bags and freeze up to 3 months. Defrost in the microwave for a couple of minutes.

Spicy Sweet Chicken Breasts

Prep + Cooking time: 5 minutes | Servings: 4

Ingredients

1 pound chicken breasts

2 tbsp garlic powder

½ cup fresh parsley, chopped

½ cup lemon juice

⅓ cup olive oil

2 tbsp stevia

Salt and black pepper to taste

2 tbsp chili flakes

Directions

Preheat the grill to 350 degrees F. In a bowl, mix the garlic powder, parsley, lemon juice, olive oil, chili flakes, salt, black pepper and stevia.

While the spices incorporate in flavor, cover the chicken with plastic wraps, and use a rolling pin to pound to ½-inch thickness.

Remove the wrap, and rub the mixture onto chicken on both all sides and toss to coat.

Place on the grill, cover and cook for 5 minutes. Baste the chicken with more of the remaining spice mixture, and cook for 5 more minutes. Let cool before storing.

Per serving

Calories 394, Fat 29g; Net Carbs 6.9g; Protein 25.5g

Storing

When cooled, divide among 4 airtight containers. Place in the fridge. You can use them for up to 3 days. To freeze, transfer to Ziploc bags and freeze up to 3 months. Defrost in the microwave for a couple of minutes.

Mediterranean Turkey Patties with Tzatziki

Prep + Cooking time: 30 minutes | Servings: 4

Ingredients

1 egg
¼ cup capers
2 garlic cloves, minced
2 green onions, thinly sliced
1 pound ground turkey
1 tbsp oregano
2 tbsp olive oil
Salt and black pepper to taste

Tzatziki

1 tbsp mint, chopped
1 garlic clove, minced
2 cucumbers, shredded and drained
1 cup Greek yogurt
2 tbsp extra virgin olive oil

Directions

In a large bowl, place the ground turkey, capers, garlic, onions, oregano, salt, and black pepper, and mix to combine. Make patties out of the mixture.

Warm the olive oil in a skillet over medium heat. Cook the patties for 3 minutes per side. In a small bowl, mix all tzatziki ingredients.

Per serving

Calories 340, Fat: 21.7g; Net Carbs: 8.6g; Protein: 27g

Storing

Refrigerate the patties and tzatziki in separate containers. Use them for up to 3 days. You can freeze only the patties up to 3 months. Defrost in the microwave and microwave for a couple of minutes, to enjoy.

Grilled Thai Chicken with Peanut Butter

Prep + Cooking time: 1 hour 50 minutes | Servings: 4

Ingredients

1 tbsp soy sauce, sugar-free
1 tbsp fish sauce, sugar-free
1 tbsp lime juice
1 tsp cilantro, chopped
1 garlic clove, minced
1 tbsp olive oil
1 tsp chilli powder
1 tsp xylitol
1 pound chicken breasts, flattened
2 oz peanut butter, melted

Directions

Combine the chicken, soy sauce, fish sauce, garlic, lime juice, olive oil, xylitol, and chilli powder in a large Ziploc bag. Seal the bag and shake to combine.

Refrigerate for 1 hour; then remove the bag about 15 minutes before cooking.

Preheat the grill to medium and grill the chicken for 7 minutes per side.

When ready, scatter with cilantro and peanut butter.

Per serving

Calories 279, Fat: 16.9g; Net Carbs: 4.8g; Protein: 25.2g

Storing

When cooled, divide between 4 airtight containers. Place in the fridge. Use them for up to 3 days. To freeze, transfer to Ziploc bags and freeze up to 3 months. Defrost in the microwave for a few minutes to enjoy.

Creamy Chicken Garam Masala

Prep + Cooking time: 45 minutes | Servings: 4

Ingredients

1 lb chicken thighs, skin removed
2 tbsp ghee
2 tbsp olive oil
1 yellow bell pepper, finely chopped
1 ¼ cups Greek yogurt
1 tbsp fresh cilantro, finely chopped
3 tbsp garam masala
2 tbsp almonds, flaked
Salt and black pepper to taste

Directions

Coat the chicken with half of the masala. Heat the olive oil and ghee in a frying pan over medium heat, and brown the chicken for 3-5 minutes per side. Transfer to a baking dish.

To the remaining masala, add yogurt and bell pepper. Season with salt and black pepper, and pour over the chicken.

Bake in the oven for 20 minutes at 400 F. Garnish with chopped cilantro and scatter with almonds.

Per serving

Calories: 382, Fat: 31.8g; Net Carbs: 3.7g; Protein: 19.6g

Storing

When cooled, divide between 4 airtight containers. Place in the fridge. You can use them for up to 3 days. To freeze, transfer to Ziploc bags and freeze up to 3 months. Defrost in the microwave for a few minutes.

Mushrooms and Green Bean Chicken

Prep + Cooking time: 40 minutes | Servings: 4

Ingredients

1 pound chicken drumsticks

2 cups mushrooms, sliced

1 cup green beans, chopped

4 tbsp ghee

Salt and black pepper, to taste

½ tsp onion powder

½ tsp garlic powder

½ cup water

1 tsp Dijon mustard

1 tbsp fresh tarragon, chopped

Directions

Warm two tablespoons of ghee in a pan over medium heat place in the drumsticks. Sprinkle with onion powder, black pepper, garlic powder, and salt. Cook each side for 3 minutes and set aside.

To the pan, melt in the remaining ghee and stir in mushrooms and beans; cook for 5 minutes until tender.

In a small bowl, mix well the mustard with water, and pour over the vegetables. Take the chicken pieces back to the pan, and cook for 15 minutes while covered. Stir in the tarragon and turn off the heat. Let cool.

Per serving

Calories 303, Fat 22.2g; Net Carbs 2.7g; Protein 21.6g

Storing

Divide between 4 airtight containers and put in the fridge. You can consume for up to 3 days. To freeze, transfer to Ziploc bags and freeze up to 3 months. Defrost in the microwave for a few minutes to enjoy.

Pork Shoulder with Paprika Sauerkraut

Prep + Cooking time: 50 minutes | Servings: 4

Ingredients

1 pound pork shoulder, cut into cubes

18 ounces sauerkraut, rinsed and drained

Salt and black pepper, to taste

1 onion, chopped

2 garlic cloves, minced

1 tbsp lard

2 tbsp sweet paprika

1 tbsp cumin

1 can (14-oz) tomatoes, chopped

2 tbsp parsley

Directions

Preheat oven to 390 degrees F.

Heat the lard in a pot over medium heat, add in the onion and garlic, and sauté for 3 minutes. Add in pork, and cook until browned.

Stir in sweet paprika and add the sauerkraut, cumin, tomatoes, and two cups of water. Cook until the meat becomes tender, for about 20 minutes.

Season with black pepper and salt. Remove to a baking dish and bake in the oven for 20 minutes.

Per serving

Calories 407, Fat 24.6g; Net Carbs 8g; Protein 32g

Storing

Divide between 4 airtight containers. Place in the fridge and consume within 3 days. To freeze, transfer to Ziploc bags and freeze up to 3 months. Defrost in the microwave for a couple of minutes to enjoy.

Bacon & Onion Pork Chops

Prep + Cooking time: 55 minutes | Servings: 4

Ingredients

2 onions, chopped

3 oz smoked bacon, chopped

½ cup vegetable stock

Salt and black pepper, to taste

4 pork chops

1 tbsp fresh sage, chopped

Directions

Cook the bacon in a pan over medium heat, until crispy, about 5 minutes, and remove to a plate.

Add onions, black pepper, and salt, and cook for 3 minutes; set aside in the same plate with bacon.

Add the pork chops to the pan, season with pepper and salt, brown for 3 minutes on each side, turn, reduce heat to medium, and cook for 7 minutes.

Stir in the stock, and cook for 2 minutes. Return the bacon and onions to the pan and cook for 1 minute. Sprinkle with the sage and let cool.

Nutritional Fact Per serving

Calories: 422; Fat: 23.8g; Net Carbs: 6g; Protein: 43.3g

Storing

Divide between 4 airtight containers in the fridge. Place in the fridge and consume within 3 days. To freeze, transfer to Ziploc bags and freeze up to 3 months. Defrost in the microwave for a few minutes to enjoy.

Roasted Pork with Swiss Chard

Prep + Cooking time: 40 minutes | Servings: 4

Ingredients

2 tbsp olive oil

Salt and black pepper, to taste

1 ¼ pounds pork loin

A pinch of horseradish powder

1 tsp hot red pepper flakes

½ tsp ground nutmeg

2 cups Swiss chard, chopped

2 garlic cloves, minced

½ lemon, sliced

1 tbsp pine nuts

Directions

Preheat oven to 400 degrees F. In a bowl, combine the ground nutmeg with salt, horseradish powder, and black pepper. Add in the meat, and toss to coat.

Heat the oil in a saucepan over medium heat, brown the pork on all sides, for 10 minutes. Transfer to a baking dish, pour in a ¼ cup of water and cover with aluminium foil.

Roast for 40 minutes, uncover and cook for 10-15 minutes more. To the saucepan, add Swiss chard, lemon slices, garlic, and 2 tbsp of water; cook for 10 minutes, and then stir in pine nuts. Let cool.

Per serving

Calories 374, Fat 22.7g; Net Carbs 3g; Protein 37g

Storing

When cooled, slice the pork and divide between 4 airtight containers, pour the swiss chard sauce over; place in the fridge Best if consumed within 3 days. To freeze, transfer to Ziploc bags and freeze up to 3 months. Defrost in the microwave and microwave for a couple of minutes to enjoy.

Mexican Chorizo with Spinach

Prep + Cooking time: 45 minutes | Servings: 4

Ingredients

1 ¼ pounds chorizo, casing removed

2 tbsp olive oil

1 onion, chopped

2 cups spinach, chopped

1 can (14-oz) tomatoes, chopped

3 tbsp tomato puree

1 tsp chipotle chili paste

4 tbsp garlic, minced

3 celery stalks, chopped

2 tbsp coconut aminos

Salt and black pepper, to taste

A pinch of cayenne pepper

2 tbsp cumin

1 tsp cilantro, chopped

Directions

Warm olive oil in a pan over medium heat. Sauté the onion, celery, and garlic for 5 minutes until tender. Add in the chorizo, and cook until browned, for about 5-6 minutes.

Stir in tomato puree, canned tomatoes, salt, black pepper, cayenne pepper, coconut aminos, chipotle chili paste, and cumin, and cook for 30 minutes while covered.

Add the spinach and cook for 3-4 minutes until wilts. Sprinkle with cilantro.

Per serving

Calories 768, Fat 61.6g; Net Carbs 7.3g; Protein 37g

Storing

When cooled, divide between 4 airtight containers. Place in the fridge and consume within 3 days. To freeze, transfer to Ziploc bags and freeze up to 3 months. Defrost in the microwave for a few minutes.

Stew Italian Sausage

Prep + Cooking time: 35 minutes | Servings: 4

Ingredients

2 onions, chopped

1 ¼ pounds Italian sausage, sliced

1 cup cremini mushrooms, sliced

Salt and black pepper, to taste

3 tbsp fresh parsley, chopped

4 green onions, chopped

¼ cup olive oil

1 cup vegetable stock

3 garlic cloves, minced

1 can (28-oz) diced tomatoes

16 ounces okra, trimmed and sliced

2 tbsp coconut aminos

1 tbsp chili sauce

1 tbsp sweet paprika

Directions

Put a pot over medium heat and warm the olive oil. Place in the sausages, and cook for 2 minutes. Stir in the onions, green onions, garlic, black pepper, mushrooms, paprika and salt, and cook for 5 minutes until tender.

Add in the chili sauce, vegetable stock, tomatoes, coconut aminos, and okra, bring to a simmer and cook for 15 minutes. Sprinkle with parsley.

Per serving

Calories 742, Fat 59.4g; Net Carbs 5.9g; Protein 26.2 g

Storing

Divide between 4 airtight containers and place in the fridge. You can use them for up to 3 days. To freeze, transfer to Ziploc bags and freeze up to 3 months. Defrost in the microwave for a few minutes to enjoy.

French Sausage Cassoulet

Prep + Cooking time: 1 hour 10 minutes | Servings: 6

Ingredients

2 tbsp olive oil

2 red onions, chopped

3 red bell peppers, seeded and chopped

2 pounds smoked sausage, sliced

Salt and black pepper, to taste

2 tbsp oregano

½ cup red wine

½ cup capers

2 pounds mushrooms, sliced

1 tbsp xylitol

Directions

Preheat oven to 390 degrees F.

In a baking dish, combine the sausage slices with xylitol, olive oil, black pepper, onion, bell peppers, salt, capers, red wine, mushrooms, oregano and a ½ cup of water.

Toss well to ensure everything is coated, set in the oven and bake for 1 hour.

Per serving

Calories 492, Fat 32.6g; Net Carbs 8.1g; Protein 33.6g

Storing

Divide the salad between 6 airtight containers and put in the fridge. You can use them for up to 3 days. To freeze, transfer to Ziploc bags and freeze up to 3 months. Defrost in the microwave for a few minutes.

Broccoli & Bacon Casserole

Prep + Cooking time: 25 minutes | Servings: 6

Ingredients

1 tbsp olive oil

2 cups vegetable broth

2 garlic cloves, minced

1 onion, chopped

1 fennel bulb, thinly sliced

Salt and black pepper, to taste

¼ cup sour cream

24 oz bacon, chopped

1 head broccoli, cut into florets

Directions

Warm olive oil in a saucepan over medium heat and sauté the bacon, garlic, onion, and fennel for about 5 minutes. Season with salt and black pepper.

Add in broccoli and vegetable broth, and cook for 15 minutes.

Stir in sour cream and let cool before storing.

Per serving

Calories 417, Fat 37g; Net Carbs 7.8g; Protein 14g

Storing

When cooled, divide between 6 airtight containers and place in the fridge. Consume within 3 days. To freeze, transfer to Ziploc bags and freeze up to 3 months. Defrost in the microwave for a few minutes.

One-Pot Meat & Butternut Squash Stew

Prep + Cooking time: 45 minutes | Servings: 6

Ingredients

1 tbsp butter

1 onion, chopped

10 oz butternut squash, chopped

8 oz spinach, chopped

1 ¼ pounds pork stew meat, chopped

2 garlic cloves, minced

4 oz red wine

1 tbsp olive oil

¼ cup xylitol

1 tbsp rosemary

1 tbsp cilantro

¼ tsp Italian seasoning

2 cups water

2 cups vegetable stock

Directions

Sauté garlic and onion in warm olive oil over medium heat for 3 minutes, until translucent.

Add the pork and cook until browned, about 5 minutes, stirring occasionally. Pour in the wine and scrape the bits that stuck to the bottom of the pot. Cook for another 2 minutes.

Add in the remaining ingredients, except for the spinach. Bring the mixture to a boil, and cook for 5 minutes.

Reduce the heat to low, cover the pot, and let cook for about 30 minutes. Stir in spinach, adjust the seasoning and cook for 3-4 minutes until the spinach is wilted.

Per serving

Calories 266, Fat: 14.9g; Net Carbs: 7.6g; Protein: 25.2g

Storing

When cooled, divide between 4 airtight containers and place in the fridge for up to 3 days. To freeze, transfer to Ziploc bags and freeze up to 3 months. Defrost in the microwave for a few minutes to enjoy.

Cheesy Beef Sausage Meatballs

Prep + Cooking time: 60 minutes | Servings: 4

Ingredients

2 tbsp olive oil

⅓ cup almond flour

1 egg

1 pound beef sausages, chopped

Salt and black pepper, to taste

¼ tsp red pepper flakes

¼ cup pecorino cheese, grated

1 onion, chopped

¼ tsp dried oregano

1 cup cottage cheese

1 cup tomato sauce

1 ½ cups mozzarella cheese, shredded

Directions

Preheat oven to 390 degrees F. In a bowl, combine the sausages, black pepper, red pepper flakes, oregano, eggs, pecorino cheese, onion, almond flour, salt, and parsley. Form balls, lay them on a greased with olive oil baking sheet, and place in the oven to bake for 15 minutes.

Remove the balls from the oven and cover with half of the tomato sauce. Pour cottage cheese all over followed by the rest of the tomato sauce. Scatter the mozzarella cheese and bake in the oven for 10 minutes. Allow the meatballs casserole to cool before storing.

Per serving

Calories 732, Fat 54g; Net Carbs 9.2g; Protein 36g

Storing

Divide the meatballs between 4 airtight containers. Place in the fridge for 3 days. To freeze, transfer to Ziploc bags and freeze up to 3 months. Defrost in the microwave for a couple of minutes to enjoy.

Beef Meatloaf with Sweet Glaze

Prep + Cooking time: 60 minutes | Servings: 6

Ingredients

1 cup zucchinis, shredded

2 pounds ground beef

2 tbsp fresh cilantro, chopped

2 garlic cloves, minced

1 onion, chopped

1 green bell pepper, seeded and chopped

½ cup pork rinds, finely crushed

⅓ cup Parmesan cheese, grated

2 eggs

Salt and black pepper, to taste

1 tsp balsamic vinegar

1 tbsp xylitol

1 tbsp worcestershire sauce

2 tbsp ketchup, sugar-free

2 cups balsamic vinegar

Directions

Preheat oven to 380 degrees F. Meanwhile, heat a small pan over medium heat, add in the 2 cups vinegar, xylitol, worcestershire sauce, and ketchup, and cook for 20 minutes.

In a bowl, combine the beef with salt, zucchini, bell pepper, Parmesan cheese, 1 tsp vinegar, cilantro, garlic, black pepper, onion, pork rinds, salt, and eggs. Set this into a loaf pan, and bake in the oven for 30 minutes.

Remove the meatloaf from the oven, spread the glaze over the meatloaf, and bake for 20 minutes. Allow the meatloaf to cool and slice.

Per serving

Calories 469, Fat 25.9g; Net Carbs 4.7g; Protein 41.7g

Storing

Divide between airtight containers. Place in the fridge and consume within 3 days. To freeze, transfer to Ziploc bags and freeze up to 3 months. Defrost in the microwave for a couple of minutes to enjoy.

Red Wine Beef Casserole

Prep + Cooking time: 30 minutes | Servings: 6

Ingredients

2 tbsp olive oil
1 ½ pounds ground beef
Salt and black pepper to taste
1 head cauliflower, break into florets
½ pound Brussels sprouts, halved
1 can (14-oz) diced tomatoes
¼ cup water
1 cup cheddar cheese, shredded

Directions

Blend the cauliflower in a food processor until it resembles rice. Warm oil in a saucepan and cook the beef for 6 minutes until no longer pink.

Add cauli rice, Brussels sprouts, tomatoes, and water. Stir and bring to boil covered for 5 minutes to thicken the sauce. Adjust taste with salt and black pepper.

Spoon the beef mixture into a greased baking dish and spread evenly. Sprinkle with cheese and bake for 15 minutes at 390 degrees F until cheese has melted and it's golden brown. Remove and cool for 4 minutes before storing.

Per serving

Calories 459, Fat 30.7g; Net Carbs 5.2g; Protein 36.7g

Storing

When cooled, divide between 6 airtight containers. Place in the fridge and consume within 3 days. To freeze, transfer to Ziploc bags and freeze up to 3 months. Defrost in the microwave for a few minutes.

Asian Beef with Green Beans

Prep + Cooking time: 30 minutes | Servings: 6

Ingredients

1 cup vegetable stock

4 tbsp ghee

2 garlic cloves, minced

1 red onion, chopped

1 tsp fresh ginger, minced

1 tbsp coconut aminos

2 pounds beef steak, cut into strips

Salt and black pepper, to taste

2 cups green beans, sliced

3 green onions, chopped

1 tbsp thai red curry paste

2 tbsp cilantro, chopped

2 tbsp sesame seeds

Directions

Cook the beef in melted ghee in a pan over medium heat, for 4 minutes. Mix in the green beans, red onion, garlic, ginger, salt, and pepper, and stir-fry for 5 more minutes.

Pour in the vegetable stock, coconut aminos, and thai curry paste, and cook for 15 minutes. Sprinkle with the green onions and cilantro.

Per serving

Calories 333, Fat 18.2g; Net Carbs 5.1g; Protein 34g

Storing

Divide between 6 airtight containers or Ziploc bags and refrigerate for up to 3 days. To freeze, transfer to Ziploc bags and freeze up to 3 months. Defrost in the microwave for a couple of minutes to enjoy.

Beef & Veggie Stew

Prep + Cooking time: 30 minutes | Servings: 4

Ingredients

2 tbsp olive oil
1 ¼ pounds ground beef
1 onion, chopped
2 garlic cloves, minced
1 can (14-oz) diced tomatoes
1 tbsp fresh dill, chopped
1 tbsp dried sage
1 tbsp dried oregano
Salt and black pepper, to taste
2 carrots, sliced
1 fennel bulb, sliced
½ small cabbage, shredded
1 cup vegetable broth

Directions

Warm the olive oil in a pan over medium heat, add in onion, fennel, and garlic, and sauté for 5 minutes.

Place in the beef, and cook for 6 minutes. Stir in the tomatoes, carrots, broth, cabbage, black pepper, oregano, salt and sage, and simmer for 15 minutes. Scatter the dill over and let cool at room temperature.

Per serving

Calories 483, Fat 30.4g; Net Carbs 6.8g; Protein 38g

Storing

Divide between 4 airtight containers. Place in the fridge. You can use them for up to 3 days. To freeze, transfer to Ziploc bags and freeze up to 3 months. Defrost in the microwave for a few minutes to enjoy.

Thyme & Carrot Bourguignon

Prep + Cooking time: 70 minutes | Servings: 4

Ingredients

3 tbsp butter

1 tbsp dried parsley

8 oz red wine

2 sprigs thyme

Salt and black pepper, to taste

1 bay leaf

5 oz vegetable stock

⅓ cup almond flour

2 lb stewing beef, cubed

4 oz shallots, halved

3 oz pancetta, chopped

2 garlic cloves, minced

1 cup mixed mushrooms, chopped

1 carrot, sliced

Directions

Melt the butter in a pan over medium heat and sauté the pancetta until slightly browned, about 5 minutes. Remove to a kitchen paper. In the pancetta fat, add the beef, season with salt and black pepper, and sear on all sides until golden, about 5-6 minutes. Set aside.

Place in shallots and garlic, and cook for 3 minutes. Stir in the carrots and mushrooms; cook for 5 minutes.

Return the beef, sprinkle with almond flour, add in the red wine and scrape the bits stuck at the bottom of the pan. Pour in the vegetable stock, and bay leaf, and return the pancetta and 1 cup of water.

Cover and cook for 50 minutes. Remove and discard the bay leaf, and sprinkle with fresh thyme.

Per serving

Calories 439, Fat 20.2g; Net Carbs 6.9g; Protein 57.3g

Storing

Divide between 4 airtight containers. Place in the fridge and consume within 3 days.

Zucchini Beef Gratin

Prep + Cooking time: 45 minutes | Servings: 4

Ingredients

2 tbsp olive oil
1 onion, chopped
1 ¼ pounds ground beef
4 zucchinis, sliced
2 garlic cloves, minced
Salt and black pepper, to taste
1 cup cheddar cheese, shredded
2 cups pecorino cheese, shredded
¼ cup pork rinds, crushed
2 tomatoes, chopped
2 tbsp dried oregano

Directions

Preheat oven to 360 degrees F. In a small bowl, mix the cheddar cheese, pecorino cheese, pork rinds, and oregano. Set aside.

Warm olive oil in a pan over medium heat, and place in the beef, garlic, salt, onion, and black pepper, and cook for 5 minutes until soft.

Remove and set to a baking dish. Add the tomatoes, and arrange the zucchini slices on top. Cover with the cheese mixture and bake in the oven for 20 minutes until brown and crispy.

Per serving

Calories 865, Fat 63.3g ; Net Carbs 6.2g; Protein 64g

Storing

When cooled, slice and divide between 4 airtight containers and refrigerate. Consume within 3-4 days. To freeze, transfer to Ziploc bags and freeze up to 3 months. Defrost in the microwave for a few minutes.

Spiced Beef Roast

Prep + Cooking time: 70 minutes | Servings: 4

Ingredients

1 tbsp olive oil
1 ½ pounds beef brisket
½ tsp garlic salt
1 tsp chili powder
A pinch of cayenne pepper
½ cup beef stock
1 garlic clove, minced
2 tsp Dijon mustard
1 tbsp mayonnaise
1 tbsp smoked paprika

Directions

In a bowl, combine the smoked paprika with mustard, mayonnaise, chili powder, garlic salt, and cayenne pepper. Rub the meat with this mixture.

Set a pan over medium-high heat and warm olive oil, place in the beef, and sear until brown.

Remove to a baking dish. Pour in the stock and garlic, and bake for 60 minutes.

Set the beef to a cutting board, leave to cool before slicing.

Per serving

Calories 397, Fat 30.4g; Net Carbs 2.3g; Protein 26.5g

Storing

Divide between 4 airtight containers. Take the juices from the baking dish, strain, and sprinkle over the meat. Place in the fridge for up to 3 days. To freeze, transfer to Ziploc bags and freeze up to 3 months. Defrost in the microwave and microwave for a couple of minutes to enjoy.

Parsley Ham Beef Stew

Prep + Cooking time: 1 hour 15 minutes | Servings: 6

Ingredients

2 tbsp avocado oil
2 celery stalks, chopped
1 carrot, chopped
1 cup diced ham
4 lb stewed beef meat, cubed
4 garlic cloves, minced
2 onions, chopped
4 cups beef stock
2 tbsp tomato paste
½ cup fresh parsley, chopped
2 tbsp ghee
Salt and black pepper, to taste

Directions

Set a saucepan over medium heat and warm avocado oil. Add in the garlic, ham, carrot, celery and onions, and cook for 5 minutes. Stir in the beef, and cook until it turns to brown.

Pour in the stock, black pepper, ghee, salt, and tomato paste. Bring to a boil and cook for 1 hour while covered. Sprinkle with fresh parsley before serving.

Per serving

Calories 673, Fat 42g; Net Carbs 6g; Protein 67.3g

Storing

When cooled, divide between 6 airtight containers. Place in the fridge and consume within 3-4 days. To freeze, transfer to Ziploc bags and freeze up to 3 months. Defrost in the microwave for a few minutes.

Butternut Squash & Beef Curry

Prep + Cooking time: 40 minutes | Servings: 4

Ingredients

3 tsp sesame oil
1 ½ pounds ground beef
1 cup beef stock
2 cup tomatoes, peeled and chopped
1 cup fresh spinach, chopped
¼ cup curry paste
1 pound butternut squash, chopped
2 bay leaves
Salt and black pepper, to taste
3 tbsp fresh parsley, chopped
1 onion, chopped
1 garlic clove, minced

Directions

Sauté the onion, garlic, and ground beef in the sesame oil over medium heat for 10 minutes. Add in butternut squash, bay leaves, curry paste, beef stock, and tomatoes, and bring to a boil.

Reduce heat and simmer for 20 minutes; season to taste. Stir in the spinach and cook for 3-4 minutes until wilted.

Remove and discard the bay leaves, sprinkle with parsley and let cool at room temperature.

Per serving

Calories 561, Fat 32g; Net Carbs 15.7g; Protein 46g

Storing

Divide among 4 airtight containers and place in the fridge. Consume within 3 days. To freeze, transfer to Ziploc bags and freeze up to 3 months. Defrost in the microwave for a couple of minutes to enjoy.

Spicy Stewed Beef

Prep + Cooking time: 1 hour 10 minutes | Servings: 4

Ingredients

2 tbsp olive oil
1 onion, chopped
1 garlic clove, minced
2 celery stalks, chopped
1 pound beef stew meat, cubed
2 red bell peppers, chopped
1 jalapeño pepper, chopped
2 green chilies, chopped
1 can (14.5-oz) diced tomatoes
2 tbsp fresh cilantro, chopped
½ cup beef broth
Salt and black pepper, to taste
½ cup capers, chopped

Directions

In a pot, brown the beef on all sides in the olive oil over medium heat; remove and set aside.

Stir-fry in the red bell peppers, celery, green chilies, garlic, jalapeño pepper, and onion, for 5-6 minutes until tender. Pour in the tomatoes, beef and broth, and cook for 1 hour.

Stir in the capers, adjust the seasoning and sprinkle with fresh cilantro.

Per serving

Calories 261, Fat 14g; Net Carbs 6.3g; Protein 27g

Storing

Divide between 4 airtight containers. Place in the fridge and consume within 3 days. To freeze, transfer to Ziploc bags and freeze up to 3 months. Defrost in the microwave for a couple of minutes to enjoy.

Coconut Lamb Kofte

Prep + Cooking time: 35 minutes | Servings: 4

Ingredients

2 tbsp coconut oil
1 ¼ pounds ground lamb
Salt and black pepper, to taste
1 ¼ tbsp coconut aminos
1 cup beef stock
¾ cup coconut flour
1 tbsp fresh cilantro, chopped
1 tbsp dried onion flakes
1 onion, sliced
¼ cup coconut cream
½ cup chicken stock

Directions

Preheat oven to 390 degrees F. In a bowl, combine the lamb with salt, garlic powder, coconut flour, onion flakes, cilantro, 1 tbsp coconut aminos, black pepper, and a ¼ cup of chicken stock. Form 4 patties, place them on a greased baking sheet, put in the oven and bake for 18 minutes.

Set a pan with the coconut oil over high heat, and sauté the onions for 3 minutes. Stir in the remaining stock, coconut cream, and the remaining coconut aminos; bring to a simmer. Remove from heat, adjust the taste.

Per serving

Calories 412, Fat 30g; Net Carbs 5g; Protein 31g

Storing

When cooled, divide the balls between 4 airtight containers and pour the sauce over. Place in the fridge. Enjoy for up to 3 days. To freeze, transfer to Ziploc bags and freeze up to 3 months. Defrost in the microwave and microwave for a couple of minutes to enjoy.

Mushrooms Stuffed with Shrimp and Parmesan

Prep + Cooking time: 56 minutes | Servings: 4

Ingredients

3 green onions, chopped

4 portobello mushrooms

2 tsp olive oil

1 pound shrimp, peeled, deveined

¼ cup chopped tomatoes

2 tbsp Parmesan cheese, grated

Salt and black pepper to taste

8 oz pork rinds, crushed

1 tbsp parsley, chopped

Directions

Preheat the oven to 370 degrees F.

Remove stems from the mushrooms and arrange them on a greased baking dish.

Warm the olive oil in a small skillet and sauté the onions and tomatoes for 5 minutes. Remove to a bowl and mix with the shrimp, half of the pork rinds, parsley, salt, and pepper.

With this mixture fill the mushrooms. Sprinkle the top with the remaining pork rinds and Parmesan cheese.Bake in the oven for 20 minutes. The shrimp should no longer be pink by this time.

Per serving

Calories 267, Fat 9.2g; Net Carbs 4g; Protein 40.7

Storing

Divide the kale between 4 airtight containers. Place in the fridge and consume within 3-4 days. To freeze, transfer to Ziploc bags and freeze up to 3 months. Defrost in the microwave for a few minutes to enjoy.

Red Cabbage Fish Taco Bowl

Prep + Cooking time: 20 minutes | Servings: 4

Ingredients

2 cups cauli rice

Water for sprinkling

2 tsp ghee

4 tilapia fillets, cut into cubes

¼ tsp taco seasoning

Pink salt and chili pepper to taste

¼ head red cabbage, shredded

1 ripe avocado, pitted and chopped

Directions

Sprinkle cauli rice in a bowl with a little water and microwave for 3 minutes. Fluff with a fork and set aside.

Melt ghee in a skillet over medium heat, rub the tilapia with the taco seasoning, salt, and chili pepper, and fry until brown on all sides, for about 8 minutes in total.

Transfer to a plate and set aside. In 4 serving bowls, share the cauli rice, cabbage, fish, and avocado. Serve with chipotle lime sour cream dressing.

Per serving

Calories 255, Fat 15.6g; Net Carbs 2.8g; Protein 25.7 g

Storing

Divide the kale between 4 airtight containers. Place in the fridge and consume within 2 days. To freeze, transfer to Ziploc bags and freeze up to a month. Defrost in the microwave for a few minutes to enjoy.

Mediterranean Cod with Tomato Sauce

Prep + Cooking time: 20 minutes | Servings: 4

Ingredients

2 tsp basil, chopped

¼ cup capers

½ red onion, chopped

4 cod fillets

1 garlic clove, minced

2 cup tomatoes, peeled and chopped

2 tbsp olive oil

1 sweet onion, chopped

2 tbsp parsley

12 kalamata olives

Directions

Sauté onion and garlic in warm olive oil over medium heat for 3-4 minutes until softened. Stir in tomatoes, bring the mixture to a boil and simmer for 5 minutes.

Add in capers and cod fillets, and cook for 8-10 minutes. Sprinkle with basil to serve.

Per serving

Calories 362, Fat: 23.6g; Net Carbs: 5.7g; Protein: 21.2g

Storing

Divide between 4 airtight containers and put in the fridge. You can use them for up to 3 days. To freeze, transfer to Ziploc bags and freeze up to 3 months. Defrost in the microwave for a few minutes to enjoy.

Dilled Creamy Salmon

Prep + Cooking time: 25 minutes | Servings: 4

Ingredients

2 tbsp olive oil
2 tbsp dill, minced
1 cup half-and-half
1 lemon, zested
Salt and black pepper to season
1 pound salmon fillets
½ cup grated pecorino cheese

Directions

In a bowl, mix the half-and-half, dill, lemon zest, salt, and black pepper.

Rub the fish with olive oil, coat it with salt and black pepper, and arrange on a baking sheet.

Spread the half-and-half mixture on each fish fillet and sprinkle with pecorino cheese.

Bake the fish for 10 minutes in the oven at 390 degrees F until the cheese is melted.

Per serving

Calories 327, Fat 32.2g; Net Carbs 4.6g; Protein 28.7g

Storing

Divide between 4 airtight containers. Place in the fridge for up to 3 days. To freeze, transfer to Ziploc bags and freeze up to 3 months. Defrost in the microwave and microwave for a couple of minutes to enjoy.

Baked Nuts Fish

Prep + Cooking time: 20 minutes | Servings: 4

Ingredients

⅓ cup macadamia nuts, chopped
2 tbsp olive oil
4 tilapia fillets
A pinch of chili pepper powder
Salt and black pepper to taste

Directions

Preheat your oven to 390 degrees F.

Arrange the fillets on a baking dish and brush with the olive oil. Season with salt and black pepper.

Sprinkle with macadamia nuts and chili powder and bake in the oven for about 15 minutes.

Per serving

Calories 255, Fat: 17g; Net Carbs: 1.5g; Protein: 24.4g

Storing

When cooled, divide between 4 airtight containers. Place in the fridge and consume within 3 days. To freeze, transfer to Ziploc bags and freeze up to 3 months. Defrost in the microwave for a couple of minutes.

Seafood Sushi

Prep + Cooking time: 10 minutes | Servings: 4

Ingredients

1 pound shrimp, cooked and chopped

¼ cup cauli rice

1 tbsp sriracha sauce

¼ cucumber, julienned

4 hand roll nori sheets

2 tbsp mayonnaise

Directions

Whisk shrimp, mayonnaise, and sriracha sauce in a bowl. Lay out a single nori sheet on a flat surface and spread about ¼ of the shrimp mixture.

Top with cucumber. Roll the nori sheet as desired.

Repeat with the rest of the ingredients.

Per serving

Calories 302, Fat: 7.5g; Net Carbs: 4.5g; Protein: 28g

Storing

Divide among 4 airtight containers and place in the fridge. Consume within 2 days. To freeze, transfer to Ziploc bags and freeze up to a month.

Celery and Salmon Packets

Prep + Cooking time: 20 minutes | Servings: 4

Ingredients

4 tbsp olive oil
1 pound salmon, sliced
Salt and black pepper to taste
2 tbsp thyme
2 oz butter, cut into 4 cubes
2 celery sticks, sliced
1 lemon, sliced
1 onion, sliced

Directions

Preheat oven to 390 degrees F and cut four pieces of baking paper, enough for each trout.

In a bowl, toss the celery and onion with a tablespoon of olive oil and share into the middle parts of the papers.

Top each with a piece of fish on each veggie mound, a drizzle of olive oil each, a season of salt and pepper, a sprig of thyme each, a slice of lemon, and 1 cube of butter each.

Wrap and close the fish packets securely, and place them on a baking sheet. Bake in the oven for 15 minutes.

Per serving

Calories 404, Fat 33.2g; Net Carbs 2g; Protein 24g

Storing

When cooled, divide between 4 airtight containers and place in the fridge. Consume within 3 days. To freeze, transfer to Ziploc bags and freeze up to 3 months. Defrost in the microwave for a few minutes.

Laksa Shrimp Soup with Cauliflower Rice

Prep + Cooking time: 20 minutes | Servings: 4

Ingredients

2 tbsp coconut oil

1 pound jumbo shrimp, peeled and deveined

2 garlic cloves, minced

2 shallots, chopped

2 tbsp red curry paste

1 cup coconut milk

Salt and chili pepper to taste

½ head cauliflower, cut into florets

2 tbsp cilantro, chopped

Directions

Blend the cauliflower in a food processor until it looks like rice; set aside.

Melt coconut oil in a saucepan over medium heat. Add in shrimp, season with salt and pepper, and cook until they are opaque, about 4 minutes. Remove to a plate.

Add the garlic, shallots and curry paste to the pan and sauté for 3 minutes until fragrant.

Stir in the coconut milk; add the shrimp, salt, chili pepper, and cauli rice; cook for 4 minutes. Reduce the heat to simmer for 3 minutes and sprinkle with cilantro.

Per serving

Calories 229, Fat 10.6g; Net Carbs 5.7g; Protein 26.2g

Storing

When cooled, divide between 4 airtight containers and place in the fridge for up to 3 days. To freeze, transfer to Ziploc bags and freeze up to 3 months. Defrost in the microwave for a couple of minutes to enjoy.

Brazilian Fish Stew

Prep + Cooking time: 25 minutes | Servings: 4

Ingredients

3 tbsp olive oil

1 cup spring onions, sliced

1 cup coconut milk

1 lime, juiced

2 diced roasted peppers

1 pound halibut, cubed

1 garlic clove, minced

2 cups tomatoes, chopped

A bunch of cilantro, chopped

Salt and black pepper, to taste

Directions

Cook spring onions and garlic in warm olive oil over medium heat for 3 minutes or until soft. Add tomatoes, halibut, roasted peppers, and cilantro. Stir-fry for 3-4 minutes.

Stir in coconut milk, and cook for 2 minutes. Do not bring to a boil. Stir in the lime juice and season with salt and pepper.

Per serving

Calories 377, Fat: 28.1g; Net Carbs: 5.9g; Protein: 20g

Storing

Divide between 4 airtight containers. Place in the fridge for up to 3 days. To freeze, transfer to Ziploc bags and freeze up to 3 months. Defrost in the microwave and microwave for a couple of minutes to enjoy.

Roasted Vegetables "Assorti"

Prep + Cooking time: 40 minutes | Servings: 4

Ingredients

4 tbsp olive oil

3 bell peppers, in different colors, sliced

1 zucchini, sliced

1 butternut squash, cut into chunks

3 shallots, halved

2 rutabagas, cut into wedges

¼ lb Brussels sprouts, halved

1 sprig basil, chopped

1 sprig thyme, chopped

4 cloves garlic, crushed

Salt and black pepper to taste

Directions

Coat the butternut squash, shallots, rutabagas, garlic cloves, brussels sprouts, zucchini, bell peppers in a large bowl with salt, black pepper, olive oil, and toss well.

Pour the mixture on a baking sheet and sprinkle with the chopped basil and thyme.

Roast the vegetables for 15–20 minutes in a preheated oven to 420 degrees F.

Per serving

Calories 363, Fat 14.5g; Net Carbs 12.5g; Protein 6g

Storing

When cooled, divide between 4 airtight containers and refrigerate for up to 7 days. To freeze, transfer to Ziploc bags and freeze up to 3 months. Defrost in the microwave for a couple of minutes.

Feta & Egg Stuffed Green Bell Pepper

Prep + Cooking time: 20 minutes | Servings: 6

Ingredients

6 green bell peppers
1 tbsp olive oil
1 ⅓ cups feta cheese, crumbled
4 eggs
1 tomato, chopped
3 tbsp parsley, chopped
1 garlic clove, minced
Salt and black pepper to taste
6 zucchini circles

Directions

Preheat oven to 390 degrees F and grease a baking sheet with the olive oil. Wash the peppers, cut off the top and deseed.

Mix all the remaining ingredients, except for the zucchini circles, in a bowl.

Arrange the bell peppers on the baking sheet and fill them with the cheese mixture. Top each pepper with a zucchini circle, pour one cup of water, and bake in the oven for 15-20 minutes.

Per serving

Calories 178, Fat: 12.3g; Net Carbs: 6.8g; Protein: 10g

Storing

When cooled, divide between 6 airtight containers refrigerate for up to 7 days. To freeze, transfer to Ziploc bags and freeze up to 3 months. Defrost in the microwave for a couple of minutes.

Cauliflower Patties with Parmesan

Prep + Cooking time: 35 minutes | Servings: 4

Ingredients

1 head cauliflower, grated
½ cup Parmesan cheese
1 red onion, chopped
½ tsp baking powder
½ cup almond flour
3 eggs
½ tsp lime juice
2 tbsp canola oil
Salt to taste

Directions

Scatter the salt over the cauliflower in a bowl, and let it stand for 10 minutes. In a bowl, mix together the remaining ingredients, except for the olive oil and lime juice.

Add in the cauliflower and mix with hands to combine.

Place a skillet over medium heat, and heat olive oil. Shape fritters out of the cauliflower mixture. Fry in batches, for about 3 minutes per side.

Remove to a plate, drizzle lime juice over and let cool completely.

Per serving

Calories 148, Fat: 13.9g; Net Carbs: 6.4g; Protein: 9.3g

Storing

Divide between 4 airtight containers and put in the fridge. You can use them for up to 7 days. To freeze, transfer to Ziploc bags and freeze up to 3 months. Defrost in the microwave for a couple of minutes.

Fried Mushrooms & Spinach Burgers

Prep + Cooking time: 15 minutes | Servings: 4

Ingredients

1 tsp mustard

2 tbsp butter, softened

½ cup asiago cheese

1 cup spinach, chopped

2 eggs, whisked

2 garlic cloves, minced

2 cups portobello mushrooms, chopped

4 tbsp almond flour

6 tbsp ground flax seeds

6 tbsp sunflower seeds

1 tbsp Italian seasoning

Directions

Sauté mushrooms, spinach, and garlic in 1 tbsp of melted butter, for 4-5 minutes until tender. Place in asiago cheese, almond flour, mustard, eggs, sunflower seeds, flax seeds, and Italian seasonings. Create 4 burgers from the mixture.

Melt the remaining butter and fry the burgers for 2-3 minutes. Flip them over with a wide spatula and cook for 3 more minutes.

Per serving

Calories 289; Fat: 22.3g; Net Carbs: 7.7g; Protein: 13.8g

Storing

When cooled, divide between 4 airtight containers or Ziploc bags and place in the fridge. You can use them for up to 3 days. To freeze, transfer to Ziploc bags and freeze up to 3 months. Defrost in the microwave and microwave for a couple of minutes to enjoy.

Baked Eggplants with Bacon & Eggs

Prep + Cooking time: 35 minutes | Servings: 4

Ingredients

1 tbsp olive oil

1 onion, chopped

2 garlic cloves, minced

4 eggplants, cut into halves

4 bacon slices

8 small eggs

Salt and black pepper, to taste

¼ tsp basil

Directions

Preheat oven to 390 degrees F and coat a baking dish with cooking spray.

With a spoon, scoop the flesh from eggplant halves, and set aside.

Fry the bacon in olive oil over medium heat for 2-3 minutes. Add in the onion, garlic, and chopped eggplant flesh and cook for 5 minutes until softened. Season with salt and black pepper.

Spread this mixture on the bottom of every eggplant half. Crack an egg in each half, sprinkle with basil, black pepper, and salt.

Arrange the filled eggplants on the baking dish and bake for 30 minutes.

Per serving

Calories 399; Fat 21.9g; Net Carbs 8.1g; Protein 18.7g

Storing

When cooled, divide between 4 airtight containers and refrigerate for up to 7 days. To freeze, transfer to Ziploc bags and freeze up to 3 months. Defrost in the microwave for a couple of minutes.

Zucchini & Mushroom Pork Sausage Cake

Prep + Cooking time: 45 minutes | Servings: 6

Ingredients

1 pound pork sausages
1 onion, chopped
1 garlic clove, minced
½ cup mushrooms, chopped
Salt and black pepper to taste
2 zucchinis, sliced
2 tomatoes, sliced
¼ cup heavy cream
8 eggs
½ cup Monterey Jack cheese, grated

Directions

Coat a baking dish with cooking spray. Open the sausages with a knife and squeeze the meat in a bowl.

Mix in the onion, mushrooms, black pepper and salt. Layer the meat mixture on the bottom of the baking dish.

Spread zucchini slices on top followed with tomato slices.

In a separate bowl, combine cheese, eggs and heavy cream, and spread this mixture on top of the veggies.Bake for 40 minutes at 370 degrees F, until the edges and top become brown. Let cool and slice.

Per serving

Calories 248; Fat: 14.9g; Net Carbs: 4.3g; Protein: 23.8g

Storing

Divide between 4 airtight containers or Ziploc bags and refrigerate for up to 3 days. To freeze, transfer to Ziploc bags and freeze up to 3 months. Defrost in the microwave for a couple of minutes to enjoy.

Crab & Avocado Boats

Prep + Cooking time: 25 minutes | Servings: 4

Ingredients

1 tsp crushed chilis
1 tsp avocado oil
1 lime, zested
8 oz crabmeat
2 avocados, halved and pitted
1 cup cotija cheese, crumbled
¼ cup almonds, chopped
2 tbsp cilantro, chopped

Directions

In a bowl, mix crabmeat with cotija cheese and lime zest. Divide this mixture between the avocado halves and top with almonds and chilis.

Bake in the oven for 15 minutes at 420 degrees F.

Decorate with cilantro and let cool.

Per serving

Calories 477, Fat: 27.7g; Net Carbs: 4.8g; Protein: 31.9g

Storing

Divide between 4 airtight containers or Ziploc bags and place in the fridge. Use them for up to 3 days. To freeze, transfer to Ziploc bags and freeze up to 3 months. Defrost in the microwave for a few minutes.

Buttery Cabbage with Feta

Prep + Cooking time: 55 minutes | Servings: 4

Ingredients

2 cups feta cheese, cubed

4 ½ tbsp olive oil

½ cup macadamia, chopped

1 tsp yellow curry powder

½ tsp onion powder

2 cups green cabbage

4 oz butter

Salt and black pepper to taste

Directions

Drizzle the feta cheese with 1 tbsp of olive oil. In a bowl, mix the macadamia, curry powder, salt and onion powder. Then, toss the feta cubes in the spice mixture. Heat the remaining olive oil in a non-stick skillet and fry the coated feta all sides; remove to a plate.

In another skillet, melt the butter and sauté the cabbage until slightly caramelized. Then, season with salt and black pepper. Remove from the heat and stir in the feta cheese.

Per serving

Calories: 677; Total Fat: 57g; Net Carbs: 7.4g; Protein: 13g

Storing

When cooled, divide between 4 airtight containers or Ziploc bags and place in the fridge. You can use them for up to 3 days. To freeze, transfer to Ziploc bags and freeze up to 3 months. Defrost in the microwave and microwave for a couple of minutes to enjoy.

Stir-Fried Tofu with Bok Choy & Pecans

Prep + Cooking time: 45 minutes | Servings: 4

Ingredients

5 oz butter
2 ½ cups baby bok choy, quartered lengthwise
2 cups extra firm tofu, pressed and cubed
½ cup pecans, chopped
Salt and black pepper to taste
1 tsp garlic powder
1 tbsp plain vinegar
2 garlic cloves, minced
1 tsp chili flakes
1 tbsp fresh ginger, grated
3 green onions, sliced
1 tbsp sesame oil

Directions

Melt half of the butter in a pan over medium heat, add the bok choy and stir-fry until softened. Season with salt, black pepper, garlic powder and plain vinegar. Sauté for 2 minutes to combine the flavors and then, spoon the bok choy into a bowl and set aside.

Melt the remaining butter and sauté the garlic, chili flakes and ginger, until fragrant. Put the tofu in the pan and cook until browned on all sides. Add the green onions and bok choy, heat for 2 minutes and add the sesame oil. Scatter the chopped pecans all over and let cool completely.

Per serving

Calories: 582; Total Fat: 52.4g; Net Carbs: 6.6g; Protein: 23.7g

Storing

Divide between 4 airtight containers or Ziploc bags and place in the fridge. Consume within 3 days. To freeze, transfer to Ziploc bags and freeze up to 3 months. Defrost in the microwave for a few minutes.

Grilled Tempeh with Cheesy Broccoli

Prep + Cooking time: 40 minutes | Servings: 4

Ingredients

Flax egg:

4 tbsp flax seed powder + 12 tbsp water

Grilled tempeh:

1 tbsp soy sauce

3 tbsp sesame oil

1 tbsp ginger, grated

3 tbsp fresh lime juice

Salt and cayenne pepper to taste

10 oz. tempeh slices

Broccoli fritters:

1 medium head Broccoli, grated

8 oz halloumi cheese, grated

3 tbsp coconut flour

½ tsp onion powder

Salt and black pepper to taste

¼ cup sesame oil

Directions

Soak the flax seed powder with water for 5 minutes.

Now, in a bowl, combine the soy sauce, sesame oil, ginger, lime juice, salt and cayenne pepper. Coat the tempeh slices with the mixture. Grill the tempeh in a grill pan over medium on both sides until golden brown and nicely smoked. Set aside.

In a bowl, add broccoli, halloumi cheese, flax egg, coconut flour, onion powder, salt and black peppe and mix the ingredients. Form 12 patties out of the mixture. Melt the butter in a skillet over medium heat and fry the patties on both sides until golden brown. Remove the fritters with the grilled tempeh to a plate to cool completely.

Per serving

Calories: 523; Total Fat: 46.4g; Net Carbs: 7.9g; Protein: 27.3g

Storing

Divide between 4 airtight containers or Ziploc bags and place in the fridge. Use them for up to 3 days. To freeze, transfer to Ziploc bags and freeze up to 3 months. Defrost in the microwave for a few minutes.

Avocado Carbonara Sauce

Prep + Cooking time: 30 minutes | Servings: 4

Ingredients

1 tsp salt
8 tbsp flax seed powder
1 ½ cups water

1 ½ cups cream cheese
5 ½ tbsp psyllium husk powder

Avocado sauce

1 avocado, peeled and pitted
1 ¾ cups heavy cream
Juice of ½ lemon
1 teaspoon onion powder

½ teaspoon garlic powder
¼ cup olive oil
Salt and black pepper to taste
4 tbsp hazelnuts, toasted and chopped

Directions

In a bowl, mix the flax seed powder with water and allow sitting to thicken for 5 minutes. Add the cream cheese, salt and psyllium husk powder. Whisk until smooth batter forms.

Line a baking sheet with parchment paper, pour in the batter and cover with another parchment paper. Use a rolling pin to flatten the dough into the sheet. Bake for 10 to 12 minutes at 300 degrees F in the oven.

Take off the parchment papers and slice the pasta into thin strips lengthwise. Cut each piece into halves, pour into a bowl, and set aside.

For the avocado sauce, in a blender, combine the avocado, heavy cream, hazelnuts, lemon juice, onion powder and garlic powder. Puree the ingredients until smooth. Pour the olive oil over the pasta and stir to coat properly.

Per serving

Calories: 719; Total Fat: 72g; Net Carbs: 6.1g; Protein: 10.3g

Storing

Place the pasta and avocado sauce in separate containers. Place in the fridge. You can use them for up to 3 days. To freeze, transfer to Ziploc bags and freeze up to 3 months. Defrost in the microwave for 2 minutes.

Coconut Flour Galette with Mushrooms

Prep + Cooking time: 70 minutes | Servings: 8

Ingredients

Tart crust

3 tbsp olive oil
1 tbsp flax seed powder + 3 tbsp water
¾ cup coconut flour
4 tbsp chia seeds
4 tbsp hazelnut flour
1 tbsp psyllium husk powder
1 tsp baking soda
A pinch of salt

Filling

1 cup mushrooms, chopped
1 cup mayonnaise
12 tbsp water
½ cup green beans, chopped
1 tsp turmeric powder
½ tsp paprika powder
½ tsp garlic powder
¼ tsp freshly ground black pepper
½ cup mascarpone cheese
1 ¼ cups Parmesan cheese, shredded

Directions

Preheat the oven to 360 degrees F.

In a bowl, mix the flax seed with the water, and let absorb for 5 minutes.

Make the crust:

Line a springform pan with parchment paper.

In a bowl, add the coconut flour, chia seeds, hazelnut flour, psyllium husk powder, baking soda, salt, olive oil, and 4 tbsp of water. Blend the ingredients with an electic mixer, add the flax seed mixture, and mix again until you obtain a dough. Spread the dough at the bottom of the pan and bake in the oven for 20 minutes.

Make the filling:

In a bowl, add the mushrooms, mayonnaise, water, green beans, turmeric, paprika, garlic powder, black pepper, mascarpone and Parmesan cheeses. Combine the mixture evenly and fill the piecrust. Bake further for 40 minutes or until the pie is golden brown. Remove, let cool and slice.

Per serving

Calories: 272; Total Fat: 24g; Net Carbs: 4.8g; Protein: 9.1g

Storing

Place the squares in a resealable container. You can store for up to 7 days at room temperature or freeze for up to 3 months. Defrost in the refrigerator.

Easter Mushroom Dumplings

Prep + Cooking time: 45 minutes | Servings: 4

Ingredients

Stuffing

2 tbsp butter
2 garlic cloves, chopped
1 red onion, chopped
1 cup mushrooms, sliced
1 fennel, thinly sliced
Salt and black pepper to taste
½ cup cream cheese
2 tbsp pecorino cheese, grated

Dumplings

1 tbsp flax seed powder + 3 tbsp water
½ cup almond flour
4 tbsp coconut flour
½ tsp salt
1 tsp baking soda
1 ½ cups pecorino cheese, shredded
5 tbsp butter
Olive oil for brushing

Directions

Preheat oven to 350 degrees F.

Melt the butter over medium heat and sauté the garlic, red onion and mushrooms, until tender; for about 5 minutes. Season with salt and black pepper and reduce the heat to low. Stir in the cream cheese and 2 tablespoons of pecorino cheese and simmer for 1 minute. Turn the heat off and set the filling aside.

To make the dumplings, in a small bowl, mix the flax seed powder with water and allow sitting for 5 minutes.

In a bowl, combine the almond flour, coconut flour, salt and baking soda.

Put a small pan over low heat, melt 1 ½ cups pecorino cheese and butter while stirring continuously until smooth batter forms. Turn the heat off. Pour the flax egg into the cream mixture, continue stirring, while adding the flour mixture until a firm dough forms.

Mold the dough into four balls, place on a chopping board, and use a rolling pin to flatten each into ½-inch thin round pieces. Spread a generous amount of stuffing on one-half of each dough, then fold over the filling and seal the dough with your fingers. Brush with olive oil, place on a baking sheet, and bake for 20 minutes or until the dumplings turn to a golden brown color.

Per serving

Calories: 454; Total Fat: 41.5g; Net Carbs: 5.9g; Protein: 12.9g

Storing

When cooled, divide between 4 airtight containers or Ziploc bags and place in the fridge. You can use them for up to 3 days. To freeze, transfer to Ziploc bags and freeze up to 3 months. Defrost in the microwave and microwave for a couple of minutes to enjoy.

Homemade Vegan Lasagna

Prep + Cooking time: 65 minutes | Servings: 4

Ingredients

2 ½ cups tofu, crumbled
3 tbsp tomato puree
2 tbsp vegan butter
1 onion, chopped
1 garlic clove, minced
½ tbsp dried basil
Salt and black pepper to taste
1 cup baby spinach

Lasagna sheets

Flax egg: 8 tbsp flax seed powder + 1 ½ cups water
1 ½ cups dairy-free cream cheese
1 tsp salt
5 tbsp psyllium husk powder

Topping

2 cups coconut cream
5 oz vegan mozzarella cheese, shredded
2 oz vegan parmesan cheese, grated
Salt and black pepper to taste

Directions

Sauté onion and garlic in the melted vegan butter over medium heat in a pot until fragrant and soft, for about 3 minutes. Now, stir in the tofu and cook until brown. Mix in the tomato paste, basil, salt and black pepper.

Pour ½ cup of water into the pot, stir, and simmer the ingredients until most of the liquid has evaporated.

Meanwhile, preheat the oven to 320 degrees F and mix the flax seed powder with the water in a medium bowl to make a flax egg. Allow sitting to thicken for 5 minutes.

Combine the flax egg with the cream cheese and salt. Add the psyllium husk a bit at a time while whisking and allow the mixture to sit for a few more minutes. Line a baking sheet with parchment paper and spread the mixture in. Cover with another parchment paper and use a rolling pin to flatten the dough into the sheet.

Bake the batter in the oven for 10 to 12 minutes, remove, take off the parchment papers, and slice the pasta into sheets that fit your baking dish.

In a bowl, combine the coconut cream and two-thirds of the vegan mozzarella cheese. Fetch out 2 tablespoons of the mixture and reserve. Mix in the vegan parmesan cheese, salt, black pepper and parsley. Set aside.

Grease a baking dish with cooking spray, layer a single line of pasta, spread with some tomato sauce, 1/3 of the spinach, and ¼ of the coconut cream mixture. Season with salt and pepper.

Repeat layering the ingredients twice in the same manner making sure to top the final layer with the coconut cream mixture and the reserved cream cheese.

Bake in the oven for 30 minutes at 400 degrees F or until the lasagna has a beautiful brown surface. Remove the dish; allow cooling for a few minutes, and slice.

Per serving

Calories: 654; Total Fat: 45.5g; Net Carbs: 7.7g; Protein: 47.1g

Storing

When cooled, divide between 4 airtight containers or Ziploc bags and place in the fridge. You can use them for up to 3 days. To freeze, transfer to Ziploc bags and freeze up to 3 months. Defrost in the microwave and microwave for a couple of minutes to enjoy.

Avocado Pesto with Grilled Tempeh & Zucchini

Prep + Cooking time: 20 minutes | Servings: 4

Ingredients

2 zucchini, spiralized

½ lemon, juiced

Salt and black pepper to taste

2 tbsp butter, melted

1 ½ lb tempeh slices

2 tbsp olive oil

Avocado Pesto

6 tbsp olive oil

1 cup Swiss chard, chopped

1 ripe avocado, halved and pitted

1 lemon, juiced

1 garlic clove, minced

2 oz almonds

Salt and black pepper to taste

Directions

Blend the Swiss chard, avocado pulp, lemon juice, garlic, and almonds in a food processor until smooth, and season with salt and black pepper.

Add the olive oil and process a little more. Pour the pesto in a bowl and set aside.

Place the zucchini in a bowl and season with the remaining lemon juice, salt, black pepper and butter.

Also, season the tempeh with salt and black pepper, and brush with olive oil. Preheat a grill pan over medium heat and cook both the tempeh and zucchini slices until browned on both sides.

Per serving

Calories: 612; Total Fat: 53g; Net Carbs: 7.6g; Protein: 37.5g

Storing

Place the pesto and grilled tempeh and zucchini in separate containers. Place in the fridge. You can use them for up to 3 days. To freeze, transfer to Ziploc bags and freeze up to 3 months. Defrost in the microwave for a couple of minutes.

Cheesy Squash Spaghetti Bake

Prep + Cooking time: 40 minutes | Servings: 6

Ingredients

2 pounds butternut squash

1 tbsp olive oil

Salt and black pepper to taste

2 tbsp butter, melted

½ tbsp garlic powder

1/5 tsp chili powder

1 cup heavy cream

2 oz mascarpone cheese

1 cup mozzarella cheese

2 oz parmesan cheese, shredded

2 tbsp fresh cilantro, chopped

2 tbsp olive oil

Directions

Cut the squash in halves lengthwise and spoon out the seeds and fiber. Place the halves on a baking dish, brush each with olive oil, and season with salt and black pepper. Bake in the oven for 30 minutes or until the pulp has softened. Remove the squash and use two forks to shred the flesh into strands.

Empty the spaghetti strands into a bowl and mix with the butter, garlic powder, chili powder, heavy cream, mascarpone cheese, half of the mozzarella cheese, and the parmesan cheese.

Spoon the mixture into the squash cups and sprinkle with the remaining mozzarella cheese. Bake further for 5 minutes or until the cheese is golden brown. Season with black pepper, cilantro, and drizzle with some olive oil.

Per serving

Calories: 342; Total Fat: 25.3 g; Net Carbs: 10.6 g; Protein: 12.3 g

Storing

When cooled, divide between 4 airtight containers or Ziploc bags and refrigerate for up to 3 days. To freeze, transfer to Ziploc bags and freeze up to 3 months. Defrost in the microwave for a few minutes to enjoy.

DESSERTS

Almond & Coconut Squares

Prep + Cooking time: 15 minutes + chilling time | Servings: 4

Ingredients

4 tbsp xylitol
¼ cup coconut oil
2 tbsp almonds, chopped
¼ tsp turmeric
10 oz coconut milk
14 oz coconut, shredded
1 tsp cardamom powder

Directions

Thoroughly combine the shredded coconut with the coconut milk, xylitol and turmeric. Let sit for 30 minutes.

Heat the coconut oil in a pan over medium heat. Add the coconut mixture and almonds, and cook for 8 minutes on low heat, mixing continuously.

Stir in the cardamom powder. Spread the mixture onto a container and freeze for 2 hours. Cut into squares.

Per serving

Calories 155, Fat: 14.3g; Net Carbs: 4.8g; Protein: 1.4g

Storing

Place the squares in a resealable container. You can store for up to 7 days at room temperature or freeze for up to 3 months. Defrost in the refrigerator.

Yogurt & Chocolate Mini Cakes

Prep + Cooking time: 45 minutes | Servings: 6

Ingredients

4 tbsp olive oil

2 cups coconut flour

1 tsp vanilla extract

⅓ cup xylitol

¼ cup cocoa powder, unsweetened

2 tsp baking powder

½ tsp salt

1 large egg

1 cup Greek yogurt

6 oz dark chocolate chips

Directions

Preheat the oven to 375 degrees F. Grease six muffin cups with cooking spray and set aside.

In a medium bowl, whisk the coconut flour, xylitol, cocoa powder, baking powder, and salt together.

In a separate bowl, whisk the egg, Greek yogurt, and olive oil, and pour the mixture gradually into the flour mixture while mixing just until well incorporated.

Gently fold in some chocolate chips and fill the muffin cups with the batter - three-quarter (¾) way up. Top with the remaining chocolate chips, place them on a baking tray, and bake for 20-25 minutes.

Remove onto a flat surface to cool completely.

Per serving

Calories 308, Fat 23.8g; Net Carbs 7.2g; Protein 5.3g

Storing

Place the muffins in a resealable container and store for up to 7 days at room temperature. To freeze, wrap each muffin freezer-safe container for up to 3 months.

Vanilla Brownies with Almonds

Prep + Cooking time: 28 minutes | Servings: 4

Ingredients

1 tbsp vanilla extract
¼ cup coconut oil, melted
4 tbsp swerve confectioner's sugar
A pinch of salt
¼ cup almond flour
½ tsp baking powder
1 egg
¼ cup almonds, chopped

Directions

Preheat oven to 350 degrees F and coat a square baking dish with cooking spray.

Pour the melted coconut oil into a bowl, add swerve confectioner's sugar and salt, and whisk to combine. Crack the egg into the bowl.

Beat the mixture until the egg has incorporated. Stir in the almond flour, vanilla extract, and baking powder.

Add the almonds, stir again, and pour the batter into the baking dish. Bake for 18 minutes until a skewer inserted into the center comes out clean. Remove and slice into brownie cubes.

Per serving

Calories 161, Fat 16.1g; Net Carbs 1g; Protein 2.3

Storing

Place the brownies in a resealable container and store for up to 5 days at room temperature. To freeze, wrap each muffin freezer-safe container for up to 3 months. Defrost at room temperature.

Coconut Fat Bombs

Prep + Cooking time: 3 minutes + cooling time | Servings: 6

Ingredients

½ cup coconut butter, melted
12 oz cream cheese cheese
1 tbsp vanilla extract
6 drops liquid stevia

Directions

Whisk the cream cheese, coconut butter, vanilla extract, and stevia with a hand mixer until creamy and fluffy, for 1 minute.

Fill into muffin tins and freeze for 3 hours until firm. Then, unmold before storing.

Per serving

Calories 310, Fat 31.6g; Net Carbs 2.3g; Protein 4.2g

Storing

Place the fat bombs in a resealable container and store for up to 7 days in the fridge. To freeze, transfer to Ziploc bags and freeze for up to 3 months.

MEASUREMENT CONVERSION TABLES

Volume Equivalents (Dry)

US STANDARD	METRIC (APPROXIMATE)
¼ TEASPOON	1 ML
½ TEASPOON	2 ML
1 TEASPOON	5 ML
1 TABLESPOON	15 ML
¼ CUP	59 ML
⅓ CUP	79 ML
½ CUP	118 ML
⅔ CUP	156 ML
¾ CUP	177 ML
1 CUP	235 ML

Volume Equivalents (Liquid)

US STANDARD	US STANDARD (OUNCES)	METRIC (APPROXIMATE)
2 TABLESPOONS	1 FL. OZ.	30 ML
¼ CUP	2 FL. OZ.	60 ML
½ CUP	4 FL. OZ.	120 ML
1 CUP	8 FL. OZ.	240 ML
1½ CUP	12 FL. OZ.	355 ML
2 CUPS OR 1 PINT	16 FL. OZ.	475 ML
4 CUPS OR 1 QUART	32 FL. OZ.	1 L

Oven Temperatures

FAHRENHEIT (F)	CELSIUS (C) (APPROXIMATE)
325°F	165°C
350°F	180°C
375°F	190°C
400°F	200°C
425°F	220°C
450°F	230°C

RECIPE INDEX

Made in the USA
Columbia, SC
17 July 2019